HIP-HOP
Biographies

HIP-HOP

RIHANNA

HIP-HOP Biographies

Chris Brown

Drake

50 Cent

Jay-Z

Nicki Minaj

Pitbull

Rihanna

Usher

Lil Wayne

Kanye West

SADDLEBACK
PUBLISHING
www.sdlback.com

ISBN-13: 978-162250-011-6
ISBN-10: 1-62250-011-3
eBook: 978-1-61247-692-6

Printed in Guangzhou, China
NOR/1012/CA21201318
17 16 15 14 13 1 2 3 4 5

Table of Contents

Timeline

1988: Robyn Rihanna Fenty is born in Barbados.

2005: Rihanna releases her first album, *Music of the Sun*. It peaks at Number Two on Billboard's Hot 100.

2003: Rihanna auditions for record producer Evan Rogers.

Rihanna moves to America to make a demo.

2006: Rihanna releases a second album, *A Girl Like Me*.

2004: Rihanna auditions for Def Jam President Shawn "Jay-Z" Carter. He signs her to the record label.

2007: Rihanna releases the album, *Good Girl Gone Bad*.

Rihanna becomes the face of Cover Girl Cosmetics and wins two awards at the MTV Video Music Awards.

2008: Rihanna wins her first Grammy Award for "Umbrella."

2009: Rihanna is a victim of domestic violence.

Rihanna releases a new album, *Rated R.*

2012: Rihanna is one of the stars of the movie *Battleship.*

2010: Rihanna wins another Grammy Award for "Run This Town."

Rihanna releases a new album, *Loud.*

Meet Rihanna

She was a little girl born on an island in the Caribbean Sea. She dreamed of singing for more than just her schoolmates and friends. She sold clothing in a street stall. But one day she would be famous enough to help children who were poor. She has been on television, in movies, and splashed across the covers of popular magazines. Who is she? She has Rihanna.

Born Robyn Rihanna Fenty, Rihanna started as an artist who sang songs that reminded people of her home, Barbados. Today, she is known for more than her singing. She has been the face of tourism for her island nation. She has sung songs for commercials and movies. She even recently became a movie star!

Her music has topped the charts in countries around the world. Rihanna has earned many awards—five American Music Awards, eighteen *Billboard* Music Awards, and five Grammy Awards. She has had eleven number one singles. She has been named the Digital Songs Artist of the 2000s decade. And Rihanna is the highest-selling digital artist in the United States.

How did Rihanna get her start? What made her sky-rocket to success at such a young age?

Rihanna arrives for an awards show in 2012.

Robyn Rihanna Fenty was born in 1988 on the island of Barbados. Barbados is an island in the eastern Caribbean Sea. The island is well-known for its beaches. Barbados is also known for cricket, its national sport. Tourists flock there because of its beauty. Barbados is bright and sunny. But Rihanna's early life was often difficult.

Rihanna's mother, Monica, was an accountant. Her father, Ronald, was the supervisor in a warehouse. Rihanna's father became addicted to crack, alcohol, and marijuana. His addictions caused problems in his marriage. It caused problems at work too. He lost his job. He tried selling clothes in a stall on the streets of Bridgetown, Barbados. Rihanna worked with him.

Rihanna grew up in Bridgetown, Barbados, an island nation with colorful buildings.

Barbados is in the Caribbean Sea, southeast of Puerto Rico.

Rihanna was a shy girl. Her singing helped her cope with her parents' bad marriage and her father's problems. She started singing when she was only seven years old. Rihanna's parents divorced when she was fourteen.

Luckily, Rihanna's father eventually stopped using drugs. Now Ronald Fenty and his daughter are very close. Rihanna says that her father inspires her. He helps her when she is troubled. She calls her father a source of strength.

During her school years, Rihanna found joy in music. In high school, she formed a trio with two of her classmates. Rihanna was also part of a group of students who trained with the Barbados military. Her drill sergeant was a singer and songwriter in Barbados named Shontelle. Shontelle has released several albums of her own. Rihanna had wanted to graduate from high school. But music had a stronger pull on her than education.

Growing up in Barbados, Rihanna was surrounded by all types of music. Rihanna listened to a lot of reggae music while she was in high school. Reggae music has a heavy beat. It sounds a lot like African music. The music is a mix of other kinds of styles called ska and mento. Reggae is most popular on the island of Jamaica. It can be heard on islands across the Caribbean and all over the world.

People around the world think of Bob Marley when they hear the word reggae. He made reggae popular in Jamaica. He was a religious leader too. Even today, Rihanna thinks of Reggae artist Bob Marley as a huge influence on her music. In fact, she has a shrine to Bob Marley in her home.

Bob Marley, a national hero in Jamaica, is one of Rihanna's heroes too.

Rihanna Is Discovered

Rihanna once said, "Music is in my DNA!" It was only a matter of time before people outside of Barbados would hear her music. She was discovered because someone took a vacation.

American record producer Evan Rogers was on a trip to Barbados. A friend of Rihanna's introduced Rogers to Rihanna. Rihanna's friend had told Rogers' wife about her singing. Rogers met Rihanna and then invited her to audition at his hotel. Rihanna brought the two other members of her trio with her. They chose to sing two popular songs. They were "Emotion" by Destiny's Child and "Hero" by Mariah Carey.

Rogers was impressed with Rihanna. He told a magazine reporter, "The minute Rihanna walked into the room, it was like the other two girls didn't exist." Rihanna made a huge decision. She left Barbados and went to Connecticut. She lived with Rogers and his wife. Her mother, Monica, came with her. Rihanna made a demo with four songs.

Rihanna was excited about her future. She was sure that she made the right decision. She explained, "When I left Barbados, I didn't look back. I wanted to do what I had to do, even if it meant moving to America."

Now she needed to get the demo done. Then she would get it into the hands of someone who could help Rihanna's career take off. Rogers discovered Rihanna, but who would help her become the famous singer she is today?

Beyoncé (center) sang with the group Destiny's Child. Later, Rihanna would meet her idol!

Rihanna was only sixteen years old when her demo was complete in 2004. It took a year to finish. Evan Rogers got Rihanna a manager. Then her demo was sent to record companies all over the world.

It did not take long for someone to respond. The first person who noticed the demo was recording artist Jay-Z. He was the president of Def Jam Recordings. After he heard the demo, he invited Rihanna to audition in his office.

Rihanna had three songs ready to sing for Jay-Z. Another person at Def Jam Records, L. A. Reid, was there too. The young singer was nervous. She explained how she felt when she walked in the room and saw Jay-Z, "That's when I really got nervous . . . I was like, 'He's right there. I can't look! I can't look!' I remember being extremely quiet. I was very shy. I was cold the entire time. I had butterflies. I'm sitting across from Jay-Z. Like, Jay-Z. I was starstruck."

Rihanna had been shaking in the lobby before her audition. But Jay-Z was impressed. He told a magazine reporter, "I signed her in one day. It took me two minutes to see she was a star." Now it was time for the rest of the world to hear Rihanna.

Rihanna is thrilled to receive an award next to her mentor, Jay-Z.

Rihanna and L. A. Reid arrive at a party before the Grammy Awards in 2007.

Barbados is a bright and sunny island. Rihanna reached back to her roots when she recorded her first album. In a way, she even named the album after her homeland. It was called *Music of the Sun*. It hit the airwaves in 2005. Even the music videos for the album reflected Rihanna's life. Rihanna explained, "Dancing was always part of my culture growing up. When I shot my first video, I worked really hard with my choreographer to perfect the routines."

The album shot up the charts. It peaked at number two on *Billboard's* Hot 100 Chart. The album went on to sell over two million copies around the world. The music had hints of reggae and Caribbean music. Many fans around the world loved the album. But critics had mixed reviews.

One magazine said that the album sounded like what Beyoncé would sound like if she had grown up in the West Indies. Another critic said that the album did not have replay value. This means that people would probably only listen to it one time. It seemed that the mix of different kinds of music and influences was hard for critics to understand. Maybe Rihanna had been too ambitious. Could she bounce back? She needed to win over the critics the same way she had won over her fans.

Rihanna performs at a holiday show in 2005.

Rihanna was very busy. After the debut of her first album, she needed to promote it. That means that she needed to sing in concerts. People would hear her music and purchase her album. She was the opening act for a very popular singer, Gwen Stefani.

At the same time that Rihanna was touring, she was recording another album. Only eight months after her first album came out, she released her second album. This album was called *A Girl Like Me*. When critics listened to the album, they liked the first single, "S.O.S." But many critics said that no other songs on the album were as good as "S.O.S."

However, the fans liked the album better than the critics. The album sold 115,000 copies in its first week. "S.O.S." became number one on the *Billboard* Hot 100. The album was number one on the Canadian Albums Chart and number five in Ireland and the United Kingdom. The second single, "Unfaithful," reached the top ten in eighteen countries around the world.

Rihanna went on tour again. This time, she did not open for Gwen Stefani or any other artist. On this tour, Rihanna was the headliner. After her *Live in Concert* tour, she went on another tour, called *Rock Tha Block*. She even toured all over Europe.

Rihanna had gained fans around the world. People packed concert halls to hear her sing and watch her dance. But would the critics ever have the same respect for Rihanna as the fans? Rihanna still had not received the critical praise that she wanted.

Gwen Stefani is an American singer, songwriter, and fashion designer. Rihanna opened for her on a concert tour.

Rihanna was known for blending Caribbean sound, dance beats, and modern words. But it was time for a change. In 2007, she decided she wanted an *edgier* look and sound. She changed her clothing. She cut her hair short and dyed it black. And she changed her sound too. Rihanna commented, "I want to keep people dancing but still be soulful at the same time. You feel different every album, and [at] this stage I feel like I want to do a lot of up-tempo [songs]."

She released her next album, *Good Girl Gone Bad*. The first single she released with her new soulful and upbeat sound was "Umbrella." Jay-Z sang with Rihanna on the song. "Umbrella" was released at the end of March 2007. It hit number one in June. Jay-Z praised the song and Rihanna's new *image*. He described the song, "It shows her growth as an artist. If you listen to the lyrics to that song, you know the depth and how far she has come."

Good Girl Gone Bad produced a hot-selling single, "Umbrella." The album debuted at number two its first week on the charts. Timbaland produced some of the *tracks*. The album even had a song that Justin Timberlake wrote for Rihanna.

She was proud of the album and excited about what it revealed about her growth. Rihanna told a magazine reporter, "*Good Girl Gone Bad* was an expression of where I am at this point in my life, where I am in my career. It just represents my rebelliousness." Fans were embracing the album. Would the critics finally like Rihanna's work as much as the fans?

Rihanna and Jay-Z perform "Umbrella" together.

The MTV Video Music Awards took place that September. Rihanna was a big winner. She was nominated for five awards, including the Female Artist of the Year.

Excitement was in the air several months later at the Grammy Awards. For the first time, Rihanna performed at an awards ceremony. The crowd cheered her on as she sang "Umbrella" and "Don't Stop the Music." But the exciting part had just begun. Rihanna, who was only nineteen years old, won her first Grammy Award. She and Jay-Z shared the award for Best Rap/Sung Collaboration for the song "Umbrella." Rihanna spoke to her father in the speech she gave when she won the award. They had had troubles when she was younger. But now, she and her dad had made peace. Rihanna gushed, "Dad, I know I promised you I'd give you my first Grammy, but we're going to have to fight for this one!"

Rihanna had finally won over the critics. She had gained new fans too. She appeared on the covers of magazines such as *Elle* and *Allure*. She released another single, "Don't Stop the Music." It reached number three on the charts.

Rihanna once said, "It is one thing to record an album, but it's a huge difference when people play it and listen to it and embrace it the way that I do. It has always been my dream to get my music out to the word and have people hear it." It seemed as if Rihanna's dreams had come true. It all happened before her twentieth birthday.

Rihanna performs live on stage during her *Loud* tour in the Netherlands in 2011.

Trouble in Paradise

After her wild success at the 2008 Grammy Awards, Rihanna was asked to perform at the 2009 awards ceremony. Her boyfriend, Chris Brown, was supposed to perform too. At the last minute, Rihanna and Chris Brown both cancelled their performances. Brown was accused of attacking a woman in his car after an argument. He had attacked Rihanna.

Brown was charged with two crimes. Later, he said in a statement, "Words cannot begin to express how sorry and saddened I am over what transpired." His apology did not sway Rihanna. She broke up with Brown because of the attack.

After the incident involving Rihanna and Chris Brown, a website showed a picture of Rihanna's bruised face. This photograph did not honor Rihanna's privacy. It also caused a problem for the police. The photograph was evidence in the case. This caused California to pass a new law. It would stop photographs like this from being shared with the public.

Rihanna did not talk about the incident for a long time. In an interview months later, she said, "This happened to me . . . It can happen to anyone." She spoke with *Good Morning, America* about the violence she had witnessed between her parents when she was a child. She explained that "[d]omestic violence is not something that people want anybody to know."

Many victims of violence were happy that Rihanna spoke about what had happened between her and her boyfriend. They thought that her story would help other people. People who had been abused might come forward to tell their stories. More people might report their abuse.

Rihanna and Chris Brown are seen here in happy times.

Even though Rihanna had faced problems with Chris Brown, she did not stop working. She appeared in a music video for a song by Kanye West. She also worked on a new song with Kanye and Jay-Z. The song, "Run This Town," won two Grammy awards. Rihanna praised her partners in the song. She said, "I just want to thank Kanye and Jay-Z for giving me the opportunity to be a part of such a wonderful song."

In 2009 Rihanna released her fourth album, Rated R. The style of her music was different from the albums she had done before. This time, the music sounded darker and more grown-up. Critics liked the album. One critic said, "Rihanna has transformed her sound and made one of the best pop records of the year." The album included singles that topped the charts in countries all over the world, including the U.S., Canada, New Zealand, and Australia.

Rihanna promoted her album with another tour. Her tour had sixty-seven shows all over the world. Rihanna had shown that she could continue to work even in the middle of problems. She said, "Keep your eyes on the finish line and not on the turmoil around you."

Rihanna sings on a German television show called "Popstars You and I" in 2009.

In the years 2010 and 2011 Rihanna worked with many other artists. She collaborated with several rappers and singers on top-selling singles.

She won two awards from her home country of Barbados, including Entertainer of the Decade. Rihanna then worked with rapper Eminem to record "Love the Way You Lie." The song reached number one on twenty-one music charts. In fact, over nine million copies of the song have been sold around the world. It was one of the best-selling songs ever.

Kanye West gathered many artists together to appear on his single "All of the Lights." Rihanna found herself in a group of famous artists, including John Legend, Alicia Keys, Fergie, and Elton John.

Rihanna released an album of her own, *Loud*, in November 2010. The album included a single that featured singer Britney Spears. That single reached number one in the

U.S. Rihanna became the youngest artist in history to have ten number one singles on the *Billboard* Hot 100.

Rihanna had come a long way from the young girl singing with two of her friends in a hotel room in Barbados. Now she was topping the charts, breaking records, and getting awards for her work.

Rihanna appears with rap artist Eminem.

Rihanna: More Than a Singer

Rihanna had had great success as a singer. But she was interested in more than just singing. Just a few weeks after releasing "Umbrella" in 2007, Rihanna had another debut. She became the face of Cover Girl Cosmetics. She appeared in print and television advertisements. Rihanna said, "It's every girl's dream to be a cover girl!"

Cover Girl was not the only company that featured Rihanna. Her song "Umbrella" could be heard in commercials for Totes umbrellas. She recorded a song for a body spray commercial too. She became a spokesperson for her home country of Barbados. Her job? To get people to visit the beautiful island nation.Rihanna even won an award in 2007 for having the "Celebrity Legs of a Goddess." She got an insurance policy on her legs for one million dollars. Rihanna told a magazine reporter that her legs were her main focus when she was exercising.

In October 2010 Rihanna released a book, *Rihanna*. She also announced that she would start her own company, called "Rihanna Entertainment." Her company would combine several different businesses. These included music, film, fragrance, fashion, and books.

Her first perfume was called "Reb'l Fleur." This translated to Rebel Flower. Rihanna introduced the perfume in 2011. She had its name tattooed on her neck. Since then, she has released two other perfumes. The name described her beauty and her edginess.

Rihanna introduces her fragrance, Reb'l Fleur.

31

Rihanna's star continued to shine. She was writing books, creating fragrances, and appearing in commercials. She also kept singing, both alone and with others. As she continued to sing, she broke records.

After Rihanna released her album *Loud* in 2010, she went on her longest tour ever, ninety-eight dates. She sold out ten nights at the O2 Arena in London, breaking another record. She had the most sold-out shows ever for a female artist.

In November 2011 Rihanna released another album, *Talk That Talk*. The lead single for the album, "We Found Love," helped Rihanna break another record. That track rose to number nine on the *Billboard* Hot 100 list. Rihanna became the fastest solo artist in the history of the chart to achieve twenty Hot 100 top ten singles. Before Rihanna, Madonna had held that record. Rihanna was only the seventh artist in history to have at least eleven number one singles. The other artists to achieve this were The Beatles, Mariah Carey, Michael Jackson, Madonna, The Supremes, and Whitney Houston. Rihanna was now in the company of superstars. On January 8, 2012, Rihanna had sold enough singles and albums to be named the best-selling digital artist of all time in the United States.

Rihanna continued to gather Grammy Awards in 2012. She won two awards for the song "All of the Lights." That brought her total number of Grammy Awards to six. Rihanna won another important award two years in a row. She was the Best International Female Artist.

Rihanna performs at the Grammy Awards.

The stage is not the only place you can see Rihanna. She has appeared in both television and in the movies.

Television has been a great place for Rihanna to show her talents. She has appeared as a guest singer on *Saturday Night Live*. She introduced challenges on America's *Best Dance Crew*. And she sat with interviewers on shows from *Good Morning, America* to *Oprah's Next Chapter*. Rihanna has appeared on *American Idol*. She was also a guest mentor on The X Factor. In early 2012, Rihanna announced that she was planning a fashion television show in the United Kingdom. Fashion designers on the show would compete to make an outfit for Rihanna to wear at a concert in London.

Rihanna has appeared in films as well as on television. First she was in a comedy about cheerleading called *Bring It On: All Or Nothing*. Rihanna had a small role as a television announcer. Two of her songs were featured in the movie as well.

Rihanna makes a fashion statement as powerful as her singing!

Most recently, Rihanna starred in the movie *Battleship*. She was a U.S. Navy officer battling aliens who have come to Earth. Rihanna watched other female movie heroes to get inspiration for her role. She described them as "...mostly actresses I looked to and looked up to and embodied their characters and tried to see how they would approach the action."

Rihanna wanted to film more movies after filming Battleship. She explained, "I didn't know if I would like it or be good at it. I really enjoyed the experience and I want to do more, try different types of roles so that I can see what I excel in most or like best."

Rihanna appears at the premier for her blockbuster movie "Battleship."

Who Influences Rihanna?

Rihanna's music has changed during her career, and she has experimented with many types of music. When Rihanna first started singing in 2005, she included a lot of reggae and Caribbean sounds in her music. That music reflected her roots in Barbados. As Rihanna grew as a performer, her music changed. Her music became less pop and sounded more like rock.

Rihanna uses a musical technique that many artists use to create music. It is called "sampling." Sampling is taking a short piece of music from a record. It is then combined with another sample in a process called "mixing." When you hear a piece of mixed music, you may be able to recognize the sample. The artist uses the sample in a new way.

Rihanna sampled a song by Soft Cell called "Tainted Love" in her song "S.O.S." Her song "Shut Up and Drive" included samples from another famous song from the 1980s, New Order's "Blue Monday." Rihanna's "Don't Stop the Music" featured music from Michael Jackson. Sampling is a way to make old music new. Rihanna chose music that inspired her to include in her new songs.

Rihanna sampled Michael Jackson's music in one of her songs.

When Rihanna was working on her album Good Girl Gone Bad, she often listened to an album called *Afrodisiac*. Brandy released the album in 2004. Rihanna described the album to a magazine, "When I was in the studio, that was the album that I listened to all the time. And I really admired that every song was a great song."

Brandy is not the only singer who influenced Rihanna. Rihanna says that Madonna is her idol and her biggest influence. She explained, "I think that Madonna was a great inspiration for me, especially on my earlier work." Rihanna also counts both Whitney Houston and Mariah Carey as inspirations for her work. In fact, Rihanna sang a Whitney Houston for her audition with Jay-Z. She sang a Mariah Carey song in a school talent show.

When Rihanna changed her image into something a bit edgier than her roots, many fans compared her to Janet Jackson. Rihanna did not mind those comparisons. She described Janet as "...one of the first female pop icons that I could relate to. She was so vibrant, she had so much energy. She still has power. I've seen her on stage, and she can stand there for 20 minutes and have the whole arena scream at her. You have to love Janet."

Brandy's music motivated Rihanna while she was making her own album.

Rihanna is excited to be part of a group of popular female artists. She explained, "There's a pack. It's me, GaGa, Katy Perry, Beyoncé . . . who else? Ke$ha for sure. Women are definitely dominating music right now, and that's because we are competitive beings. I feel like music hasn't been this exciting in a while."

Rihanna counts Janet Jackson among her musical influences.

Throughout her career, Rihanna has changed and grown as an artist. Her look has changed as well. She replaced her longer flowing island dresses to shorter, tighter leather outfits. She changed her hair to a cropped style. Some people consider Rihanna to be a fashion icon. Rihanna explained her own personal style, "When I am putting looks together, I dare myself to make something work. I always look for … something that's a little off, but I have to figure it out. I have to make it me. I think that's the thrill of fashion."

Rihanna put great outfits together. She has also worked with designers to create clothing for others to wear. She worked with top fashion brand Armani to create clothing for their new collections in fall 2011 and spring 2012. Rihanna announced that she was going to start her own fashion line. She wanted to work with other designers to create new clothes. She said, "I'm working with designers I respect. I want people to trust me before I say, 'Buy it because it's mine.'"

In July 2012 Rihanna announced her first collection for a company called River Island. The clothes would hit the stores in the spring of 2013. Rihanna was excited to work with the London-based store. She said, "River Island is the perfect partner for me to collaborate with. I find London really inspiring and River Island loves to have fun with clothes. I'm looking forward to working with them and creating something really special."

As Rihanna's singing has changed, her image has changed too.

Rihanna Gives Back

Growing up in Barbados, Rihanna often saw children who were poor. She remembered those images when she grew up and became a celebrity. Rihanna explained, "When I was young and I would watch television and I would see all the children suffering, I always said: when I grow up, I want to help." Rihanna has helped many charities.

In 2006 Rihanna started the Believe Foundation. The goal of the foundation is to help children who are ill so that they can have a future. The foundation gives school supplies, toy, clothes, and medical attention to children in need. One of its goals is to register people to be bone marrow donors so that they can save children with leukemia, which is a cancer in the blood.

The foundation needs money. One way that Rihanna has raised money is to give concerts. After the concerts, she meets the children who attend. She signs autographs and poses for pictures with fans.

Rihanna believes in helping charities that focus on many different needs. She performed for a fundraiser for Africa. She supports organizations that focus on AIDS, relief for disasters, and issues that have to do with protecting the environment. She sang at a concert to raise money for young cancer victims.

She also performed at Jay-Z's "Answer the Call" concert, which honored firefighters and police officers who died on September 11, 2001. Rihanna designed clothing for a collection called Fashion Against AIDS. The clothing makes teens more aware of issues about AIDS.

Rihanna even became the official face of tourism for her home country of Barbados. February 20, 2008, was officially "Rihanna Day" in Barbados.

Rihanna signs autographs for her many young fans.

Rihanna is a singing sensation, a writer, a designer, an activist. What will Rihanna do next?

In March 2012 Rihanna said that she wanted to take a break from recording new music. Instead, she wanted to work with other artists and create videos. After the premiere of *Battleship*, she wanted to appear in other movies.

After the premiere, Rihanna explained that she was working on a sound for a new album. She said, "I love experimenting and I love working with different sounds and putting them together so that they're not so one-dimensional." She also planned to go on a tour in 2013, larger than any other tour she has done before.

Rihanna once described herself, "I like to be creative." Her creativity shows in all that she has done so far. Rihanna also wants to enjoy all that she does. She explains, "When you realize who you live for, and who's important to please, a lot of people will actually start living. I am never going to get caught up in that. I'm gonna look back on my life and say that I enjoyed it—and I lived it for me." While Rihanna lives life for herself, her many fans will certainly enjoy it as well!

Rihanna performs during the results show for Fox's "American Idol" in May 2012.

Vocabulary

addicted	(adjective)	dependent on something habit-forming, such as drugs or alcohol
ambitious	(adjective)	wanting to achieve success, power, wealth, or another goal
audition	(verb)	to try out in front of judges
Billboard	(noun)	magazine that covers the music industry, including record and album sales
choreographer	(noun)	a person who plans dance moves
collaboration	(noun)	something that is created working with another person
cope	(verb)	to deal with a problem or difficulty
crack	(noun)	an illegal drug made from cocaine
critics	(noun)	people who judge
demo	(noun)	a sample, especially of a song, to introduce people to the musician
digital	(adjective)	electronic, such as on a computer, MP3, or other electronic device
DNA	(noun)	a set of traits or characteristics of a person or thing
domestic violence	(noun)	violence against a person living in your own home or very close to you
edgy	(adjective)	innovative or new
Grammy Award	(noun)	an award given to the best recording artists every year by The Recording Academy
headliner	(noun)	a performer whose name appears before others; a star

icon	(noun)	a person who stands as a great example
influence	(noun)	a person or thing that is a force on others' beliefs, actions, or behaviors
inspiration	(noun)	someone or something that motivates or spurs on
mentor	(noun)	someone who teaches or trains others
nominate	(verb)	to suggest that someone might deserve an award
pop	(noun)	music that is generally appealing; a watered-down version of rock and roll
review	(noun)	a report, a critique, or an evaluation
shrine	(noun)	a structure or a place that honors someone or something
sign	(verb)	sign a contract
single	(noun)	one song, usually from an album
spokesperson	(noun)	a person who speaks for another person or a group
stall	(noun)	a booth or stand used to display merchandise, or things for sale
track	(noun)	a song on a record
transform	(verb)	change
trio	(noun)	a group of three
turmoil	(noun)	great confusion, disturbance, tension, or nervousness

Photo Credits